PAPER
QUILLING
ADORABLE
ANIMALS

PAPER QUILLING
ADORABLE ANIMALS
Chinese Style

By Zhu Liqun Paper Arts Museum

Better Link Press

On page 1
Fig. 1   *Carp Leaping over the Dragon Gate*
"Carp leaping over the Dragon Gate," a phrase used to describe the pioneering spirit of hard work and forging ahead, is taken from a folktale in ancient China. The Dragon Gate is set in the Yellow River Valley. According to the legend, the turbidity of the Yellow River made it impossible for fish to survive, except for the pollution-resistant carp, which thrived in the rough waters. Every spring, these golden carps swam against the current, forming a jumping colony in the Dragon Gate. It's said these golden carps would change into dragons after jumping over the Dragon Gate. This work depicts a lively picture of a school of carps trying to cross the Dragon Gate.

On pages 2–3
Fig. 2   *The Richness of Gold and Jade*
In Chinese traditional auspicious patterns, a pool of goldfish is often used to represent being rich in gold and jade. In this work, the author creates two carefree goldfish swimming in the pool, foregrounding the auspicious atmosphere in a free style.

For Zhu Liqun Paper Arts Museum
Project Designers: Zhu Liqun, Yao Xiaoyan
Text and Photographs: Wang Chenbo
Works: Zhu Liqun, Yao Xiaoyan, Liu Xiuxia, Qian Ciying, Wang Chenbo, Zhu Jiayan, Yan Wenjun, Chen Boyu, Qian Caidi, Ding Yijun, Zhang Junping, Xue Suomei, Li Chengxin
Technique Demonstration: Zhu Jiayan

Translation: Shelly Bryant
Cover Design: Wang Wei
Interior Design: Li Jing, Hu Bin (Yuan Yinchang Design Studio)

Editor: Cao Yue
Editorial Director: Zhang Yicong

Senior Consultants: Sun Yong, Wu Ying, Yang Xinci
Managing Director and Publisher: Wang Youbu

ISBN: 978-1-60220-609-0

Address any comments about *Paper Quilling: Adorable Animals* to:

Better Link Press
99 Park Ave
New York, NY 10016
USA

or

Shanghai Press and Publishing Development Co., Ltd.
F 7 Donghu Road, Shanghai, China (200031)
Email: comments_betterlinkpress@hotmail.com

Printed in China by Shanghai Donnelley Printing Co., Ltd.

1   3   5   7   9   10   8   6   4   2

Fig. 3   *Landscape Series (Picture One)*
Landscapes are one of the most important themes of Chinese painting, and also an important image in traditional Chinese culture related to auspiciousness. Landscapes symbolize one's noble character and magnificent career. In this series of five pictures of mountains and rivers, the artist uses paper instead of brushes, drawing on the forms of mountains, rocks, and flowing water in landscape paintings to depict landscapes with different characteristics, presenting crystal rivers and verdant mountains, grotesque and rugged rocks, or high mountains and murmuring water.

CONTENTS

Top
Fig. 4   *Independent Hero*
In traditional Chinese patterns, an eagle standing alone on a cliff often implies a unique heroic figure. This work depicts an eagle standing proudly on a cliff. This eagle is majestic, commanding, and ready to fly in the sky with open wings. Its composition is momentous.

CONTENTS

On facing page
Fig. 5   Paper strips.

Top
Fig. 6   *Dragon*

PREFACE

W e should learn from our children, especially from their curious, unrestrained approach to exploring change when they play with toys. They will not be satisfied with established results. What attracts them most is the toys that can be disassembled and reassembled according to their own preferences. The intellectual toy "tangram" (a puzzle composed of seven boards), handed down from ancient times, consists of nothing more than five triangular boards and two quadrilateral boards, but together these simple boards produce kaleidoscopic graphics. The process of playing the seven-piece puzzle forms in us an awareness that seemingly complex things can be reduced to the simplest elements by decomposition, and simple elements can be combined into extremely rich alterations.

We have compiled two books of "quilling art," in which we encourage quilling art enthusiasts to exercise a spirit of variety, so that learning becomes an exploratory process of exerting personality. In this book, we will further present the principle of change through the simplest items. The parts of various shapes in these works are derived from the simplest elements of different sizes and lengths, with the longer ones turning into lines and the smaller ones into dots, and both merging into a plane. You will find the art of paper quilling amazingly simple.

Learning paper quilling is like playing with toys, exploring with curiosity, and combining with imagination. You do not need to stick to the book's view. Rather, you should leave space for your own ideas. Everyone is sure to find paper quilling a surprisingly interesting art.

Zhu Liqun

On facing page

Fig. 7   Crane

In traditional Chinese culture, the crane is a symbol of auspiciousness, longevity, and elegance. In Taoism, the crane is often used as an immortal's mount because of its ethereal grace. This work is ingeniously presented in a round composition, with the orange sunlight and blue waves dividing the picture into two, vividly highlighting a flying crane and creating a scene of elegance and profundity.

INTRODUCTION

*P*aper quilling is a type of craftwork produced by splicing and stacking long, colorful paper strips, turning them into various basic elements through processing by hand or with simple tools. Using paper as the carrier of artistic expression, paper quilling includes various techniques, different styles, unique charm, and unlimited potential for artistic expression.

Originating in the West, paper quilling has been welcomed by more paper art enthusiasts since its introduction into China. With their distinctive wisdom, creativity, and dexterity, Chinese enthusiasts have given new life to paper quilling and brought new changes and possibilities to this traditional Western art form. Zhu Liqun Paper Arts Museum is the first paper quilling art studio in China. Under the leadership of artist Zhu Liqun, a group of paper art enthusiasts have worked together to integrate traditional Chinese culture and artistic expressions into this art form, creating paper quilling with Chinese characteristics.

Chinese style paper quilling applies flexible techniques, expresses rich themes, and highlights a free style of creation. With some simple basic skills, beginners are able to create their own paper quilling works and experience unparalleled fun in the process.

On facing page

Fig. 8 *God of Longevity*
The long-lived man is the God of Longevity in ancient myth. In this work, the author skillfully uses a large number of crescent elements, showing his big forehead, long eyebrows and beard, and ripe pink peaches, vividly capturing the image of a smiling old man enjoying a long life.

Fig. 9 *Carp Leaping over the Dragon Gate*
In this work, the artist uses blue crescents to represent the waves of the Yellow River and green splashes to show the turbulence of the current. Two carps, one golden and one red, are working hard to go upstream, refusing to give up. It is another expression of "carp leaping over the Dragon Gate."

CHAPTER ONE

Chinese Style Paper Quilling and Chinese Auspicious Culture

*I*nheritance and innovation are the greatest characteristics of Chinese style paper quilling. Compared with the traditional Western style, the outstanding feature of Chinese paper quilling is that it absorbs traditional Chinese culture and draws upon traditional Chinese art forms to create novel techniques and express the art of paper quilling in a free, changing, and flexible style. In this book, we choose quilling works with auspicious themes, focusing on the animals that people have favored to present the unique artistic beauty of Chinese style paper quilling.

Auspicious culture has a long history in China, carrying the Chinese people's yearning for a better life and their prayerful visions. Every country or nation has its own customs, culture, and beliefs, giving birth to different forms and expressions of auspicious culture. It is generally believed that the auspicious culture of China originated from the symbols and totems depicted in ancient people's sacrifices. Totems are the oldest form of mascots. Ancient people believed that totems had the power to eliminate disasters and safeguard peace. In the Shang and Zhou dynasties (1600–256 BC), people began to cast patterns on the bronze wares used for celestial worship or ancestor worship in their prayers for good fortune and avoidance of misfortunes, which embodies China's auspicious culture. During the Warring States period (475–221 BC), the connotation of auspicious culture was further developed, and more mascots with symbolic significance emerged. With the progression of history, people's awareness of auspiciousness and those auspicious symbols have gradually developed into China's traditional auspicious culture.

Auspicious culture can be divided into different categories based on its sources and carriers, and the criteria for classification are not conclusive. The paper quilling works in this book include categories such as zodiac, mythical

On facing page
Fig. 10 *Landscape Series* (Picture Two)
See page 4 for details.

Fig. 11 *Pixiu*

In Chinese mythology, the Pixiu is one of the nine sons of the dragon. It is a winged, lion-like beast, which symbolizes benevolence and auspice. It can guard treasures and drive away monsters and evil spirits. This work employs simple colors and exquisite techniques to create a majestic Pixiu.

creatures, animals, homophony, landscapes and figures.

Auspicious zodiac is made up of the twelve zodiac animals, which are applied to record people's year of birth. These twelve species of animals match the twelve earthly branches in traditional Chinese cosmology. Their status and influence in China are similar to those of the twelve constellations in the West. In Chinese people's heart, these twelve animals are auspicious, and they have been endowed with positive personality traits.

Auspicious mythical creatures include the unicorn, phoenix, tortoise and dragon, the four legendary sacred beasts, respectively representing benevolence, dignity, longevity, and holiness. For thousands of years, Chinese people have held these four sacred beasts as mascots. The Chinese nation refers to itself as "the descendant of the dragon," which reveals the high position of the dragon among Chinese people (Fig. 11).

Auspicious animals are those animals found in nature, which the imaginative Chinese people have endowed with unique meanings. Cranes, magpies, peacocks, white tigers, spiders, etc. are all auspicious animals in the hearts of Chinese people.

Auspicious homophony is built on the Chinese monosyllabic characters. There is a large number of Chinese characters with the same pronunciation, making the Chinese homophonic culture much richer than other languages. For example, *fu* is pronunciation of both the characters of "bat" and "luck"; pronunciation *lu* or "deer" is a homophone for "fortune," and *hou* or "monkey" is a homophone for "nobility." The combination of multiple homophonic characters can produce new implications, as explained in the works *Heron (for Success)*, *Cat and Butterfly (for Wellness)* and *Elephant (for Peace)*.

There is also **auspicious landscapes**, which is an important part of traditional Chinese culture, where the landscape occupies a prominent position. It is not only a significant theme of poetry and painting by the literati, but also the most typical image in Chinese geomancy. In ancient China, according to the trends of mountains and rivers, people summed up the three main dragon veins of China, believing that they affected the destiny and future of the entire people and nation. The mountains and waters are spiritual, and it is believed that there are immortals on the mountains and dragons in the waters. Therefore, the mountains and waters are viewed as the incarnations of the gods to be worshipped by believers. Many Chinese people like to hang landscape paintings in their offices to seek smooth sailing or fortune, or to remind themselves of the spirit and mind of high mountains and great rivers. It can be said that mountains and rivers are the biggest mascots in traditional Chinese auspicious culture (Fig. 13).

Fig. 12 *Bole Identifying Excellent Horses*
According to legend, Bole lived in the Spring and Autumn period (770–476 BC) and was skilled in identifying excellent horses. Since then, the phrase "Bole Xiangma" has come to refer to one who is skilled in identifying and selecting talent. In this work, the author combines the image of Qianlima (a good horse) and Bole, showing the attentiveness of Bole as he identifies the good horse and the joy of Qianlima when it meets Bole.

Auspicious figures in Chinese culture have a wide range of sources. These come from ancient myths, such as Pan Gu and Nü Wa; from the origin of the Chinese nation, such as Emperor Yan and Emperor Huang; from Taoist legends, such as Jade Emperor, the three stars of Luck, Fortune, and Longevity; from Buddhist classics, such as Guanyin and Maitreya; or from real historical figures, such as Confucius (551–479 BC) or general Guan Yu (?–220). These auspicious figures are popular among the Chinese people, and they have been handed down from generation to generation, continuing for thousands of years (Fig. 12).

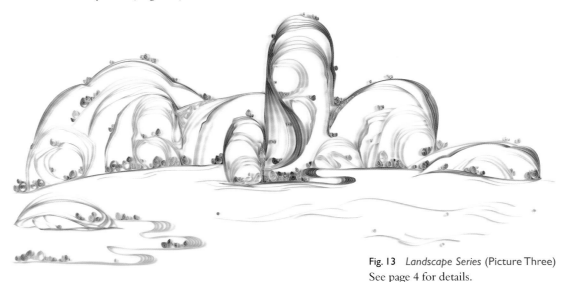

Fig. 13 *Landscape Series* (Picture Three)
See page 4 for details.

CHAPTER TWO
Preparation of Paper Quilling

*T*his chapter covers the preparation that must be understood before the creation of paper quilling works, including materials, tools, techniques, and basic elements. Paper is the carrier of quilling art, and thus the most important material. The texture, color, and width of the strips are key to the success of the work. The creation of Chinese style paper quilling does not rely heavily on special tools; some simple tools can be used to make the production process more efficient. "Ten Basic Techniques" is the summary of the techniques used in the creation of Chinese paper quilling art, which can help you get on the path to creation as soon as possible. The introduction of basic elements will enable you to learn how to make the basic elements of Chinese style paper quilling systematically.

On facing page

Fig. 14 *Happiness on the Plum Tree*

In traditional Chinese auspicious patterns, magpies flying to the top of plum trees are often depicted as an emblem of "happiness on the eyebrow" (referring to the expression of joy captured in eyebrows wrinkled in a smile. "Magpie" is homophonic with "happiness" and "plum" is homophonic with "eyebrow.") In this work, the artist depicts two magpies resting on the double Chinese character *xi* (happiness) amidst the plum blossoms. The overall picture is ingenious in composition, bright in color, and joyful in style.

Fig. 15 *Good Fortune and Peace*

In traditional Chinese culture's focus on auspiciousness, the elephant symbolizes auspiciousness, and an ear of grain embodies prosperity. In this work, the author creates an adorable elephant carrying a large stack of grain on its back. The brocade pattern on the elephant includes the Chinese character "auspice," which embodies good wishes for one's life.

1. Materials

With the popularity of the art of paper quilling, you can easily get specialized strips of paper quilling at brick-and-mortar or online stores. In fact, you can also select paper of various textures and colors according to your preferences and cut it into strips. It should be noted that the selected paper should have certain plasticity and elasticity, with moderate thickness, or it may weaken the artistic expression of paper quilling.

The width of paper strips used for different paper quilling works also varies. Most of the works in this book use 5-mm-wide strips, which are moderate and fit for most Chinese style paper quilling works. In addition, in some works, the authors use 1.5-mm and 3-mm-wide strips to make smaller elements to present the details better. In large-scale works, we can also choose 1-cm-wide or even wider strips to match the scale of the work, enabling it to stand out.

In terms of the selection of the background paper, there is no definite stipulation in Chinese style paper quilling. You can select it based on personal preference. White watercolor paper is mostly used in the works introduced in this book.

2. Tools

The tools for Chinese style paper quilling are simple and flexible. In addition to those introduced below, you can exercise your imagination to locate the

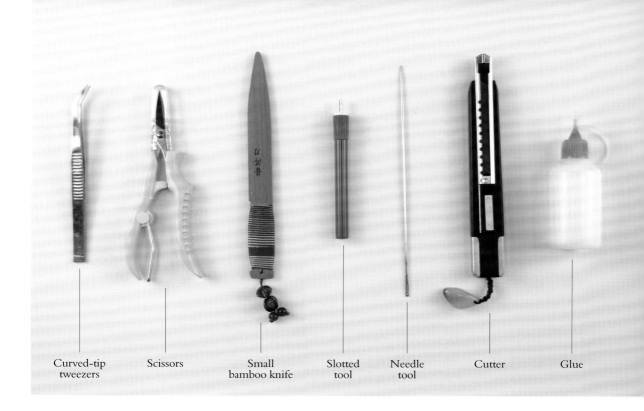

Curved-tip tweezers   Scissors   Small bamboo knife   Slotted tool   Needle tool   Cutter   Glue

tools in daily life for your creative work.

Curved-tip tweezers are used to accurately grip, place, and fix smaller elements.

Scissors are used to trim the excess part of the strips.

Small bamboo knife frequently used in this book is actually a tea knife, which is for loosening up Pu'er or other tea cakes. It is small, portable and safe, suitable for smoothing and scraping the paper strips. You can also find a similar handy tool at home.

Slotted tool is the most commonly used tool for traditional Western-style paper quilling. It is used especially for scrolling strips. Its front end has a slot, into which the strip is inserted and shaped by rotating the tool. You can also use the thick end of the tool to scroll the paper.

Needle tool (or toothpick) is dipped in glue and applies glue to the strip precisely to make the work neat and tidy.

Cutter is used to cut paper and strips.

Glue is used to fix the strips and the elements of the work onto the background paper.

You can choose tools based on what you need, or pick tools other than those tools mentioned above. When you become skillful in the techniques, you may reduce the use of tools, relying more on your hands to create the works. In addition, it is not advisable to use paper templates in Chinese style paper quilling. The template may make it easier to create the elements, but it will limit the freedom, flexibility, and variety of your works.

3. Ten Basic Techniques

Smoothing: Hold one end of a strip with the thumb and forefinger of the left hand, then press the bamboo knife in the right hand against the reverse side of the strip. Put the right thumb on the front side of the strip and smooth the strip from head to tail. This can help the strip present softer curves, with more plasticity for further modeling.

Smoothing

You can also do it without a knife, use your right forefinger and thumb to attach the two sides of the strip, smoothing it from head to tail a couple of times to achieve the same effect.

Scraping: This is similar to smoothing. With a small bamboo knife, one needs to press the thumb more tightly against the knife and scrape the strip very hard. Without tools, one needs to use greater force with the thumb and the forefinger. This will allow the strip to bend into strong, natural curves.

Scraping

The difference between scraping and smoothing lies in the degree of force and the stages of creation, with the former used as preparation before shaping, while the latter is skillfully employed as part of shaping.

Bending: Bend the strip with both hands into various curves to meet the needs of the shape.

Scrolling: Scroll the strips with slotted tool or other small cylinders to form coils. This is the most basic and important technique in paper quilling. When you become familiar with the technique, you can simply use your hands without the aid of tools.

Bending

Pulling: Stack several strips and glue the starting ends, then gently pinch the middle part with one hand and pull the strips out to varying lengths with the other hand to create your desired shape. This technique is mostly used for crescent elements.

Pasting: Use glue to fix and paste the shaped strips into basic elements and attach

Scrolling

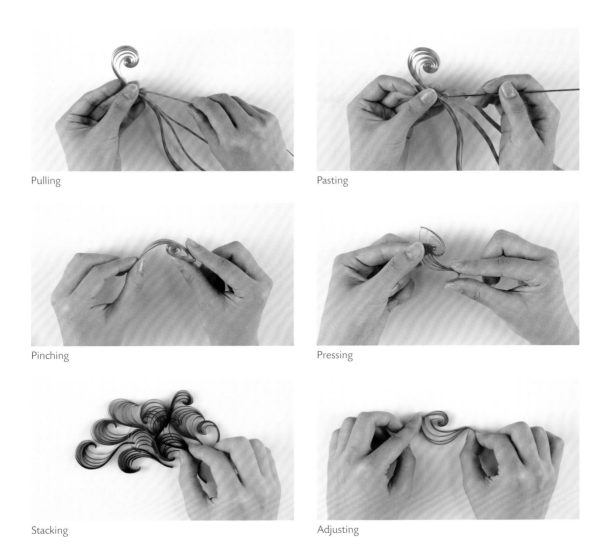

Pulling

Pasting

Pinching

Pressing

Stacking

Adjusting

the elements to the background paper. The amount of glue and the skill determine whether the basic elements are pleasant to the eye and the proper placing determines the overall effect of the work. Do not overlook pasting due to its simplicity.

Pinching: After scrolling the strip, pinch it into sharp angles at one or more positions of the coil with the thumb and the forefinger, which allows the coil to present varying shapes.

Pressing: Press strips or scrolls with the thumb and the forefinger at the same time to create the desired shape.

Stacking: Stack together a couple of basic elements, so that when the second or third layers were appropriately placed, the picture will present more dimensions and perspectives.

Adjusting: Adjust the basic elements, lines, shapes, compositions, and pictures to generate best effect.

4. Basic Elements

Compared with traditional Western paper quilling works, which heavily use coil elements, Chinese style paper quilling has initiated more categories of elements. In Chinese style paper quilling, the elements of line, scroll, loop, coil, and crescent complement each other, presenting free, changing, and flexible styles of creation.

Line and Scroll

In Chinese style paper quilling, a line is not only the initial state of a strip before it is shaped, but also one of the most basic elements. A scroll is a spiral curve produced when a strip is scrolled up and loosened.

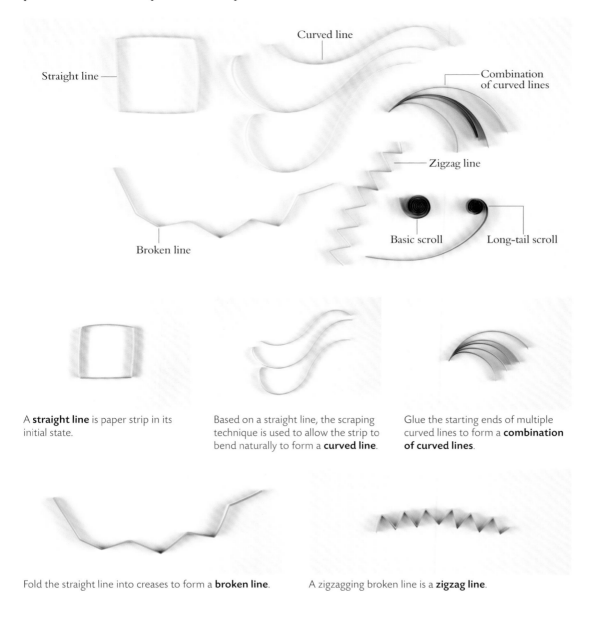

Curved line

Straight line

Combination of curved lines

Zigzag line

Broken line

Basic scroll

Long-tail scroll

A **straight line** is paper strip in its initial state.

Based on a straight line, the scraping technique is used to allow the strip to bend naturally to form a **curved line**.

Glue the starting ends of multiple curved lines to form a **combination of curved lines**.

Fold the straight line into creases to form a **broken line**.

A zigzagging broken line is a **zigzag line**.

Scroll up and loosen a strip with a slotted tool to form a **basic scroll**.

When the strip is scrolled, a length of the strip is left undone to form a tail, this is a **long-tail scroll**.

Coil

The coil is the most common element in traditional Western paper quilling works. Various shapes can be formed by scrolling, pinching, and pressing the loose coils.

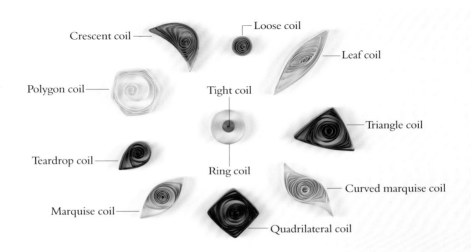

Crescent coil

Loose coil

Leaf coil

Polygon coil

Tight coil

Triangle coil

Teardrop coil

Ring coil

Curved marquise coil

Marquise coil

Quadrilateral coil

Take a piece of strip, scroll up the starting end with slotted tool and then loosen it.

Cut out the excess part and glue the tail end.

A **loose coil** is completed.

When the strip is scrolled more tightly, a **tight coil** is formed.

A **ring coil** forms when the inner part is hollow while the outer is tightly scrolled.

Pinch one end of the loose coil to form a **teardrop coil**.

Pinch the opposite ends of a loose coil with both hands to form a **marquise coil**.

When pinching the marquise coil, move one hand upward and the other downward, causing the marquise coil to twist and warp into a **curved marquise coil**.

On the basis of a marquise coil, pinch the middle of the marquise coil flat to form a **leaf coil**.

Pinch three pointed corners out of the loose coil to form a **triangle coil**.

Pinch four corners out of the loose coil to form a **quadrilateral coil**.

Pinch more corners out of the loose coil to form a **polygon coil**.

Pinch the loose coil into a crescent shape to form a **crescent coil**.

Loop

A strip or strips of paper are looped, with the ends of the strips glued together. The loop element is smooth in line, and rich and abundant in shape, usually acting as structural elements.

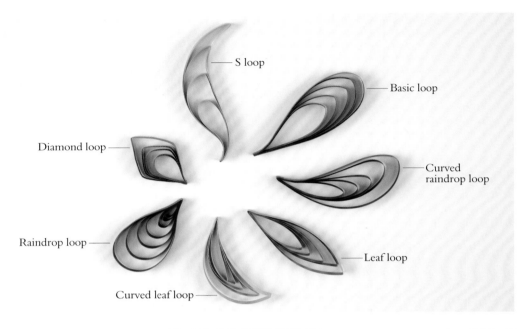

S loop

Basic loop

Diamond loop

Curved raindrop loop

Raindrop loop

Leaf loop

Curved leaf loop

Take several strips of paper and glue their starting ends together.

Smooth the strip with a small bamboo knife.

Form the strips into a loop, and draw the strips from the tail ends in different lengths to present different dimensions.

Paste the tail ends with glue, and then paste the starting end and the tail end, trim excess strips to form a **basic loop**.

On the basis of the basic loop, adjust the shape to make it a full, round **raindrop loop**.

Bend the raindrop loop to form a **curved raindrop loop**.

Pinch one end of the basic loop to form a **leaf loop**.

Bend the leaf loop to form a **curved leaf loop**.

Scrape the two ends of the basic loop with a small bamboo knife to form an **S loop** similar to the S crescent.

Pinch the basic loop into a diamond to form a **diamond loop**.

Crescent

The crescent element is unique to Chinese style paper quilling, which best presents the characteristics of the Chinese style. Its lines are neat and beautiful, its shapes elastic and changeable, and its applications flexible and casual.

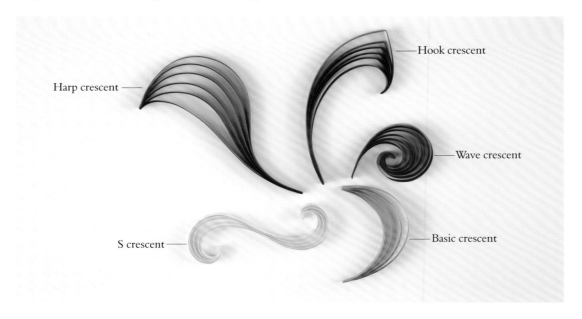

Hook crescent

Harp crescent

Wave crescent

S crescent

Basic crescent

Take several strips and glue their starting ends together.

Smooth the paper with a small bamboo knife.

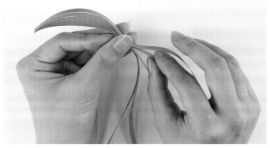

Hold the strip in the middle with one hand and pull the strip out in varying lengths with the other hand.

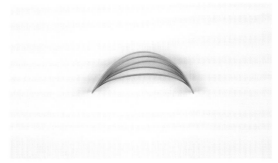

Paste with glue, cut out the excess part to form a **basic crescent**.

When making a crescent, scroll up the starting end of the basic crescent with a slotted tool to allow the crescent to bend heavily into a **wave crescent**.

Fold in the middle of the basic crescent to form a **hook crescent**.

Make a slim basic crescent, and scrape its tail ends in an opposite radian with a small bamboo knife to form an **S crescent**.

Based on the basic crescent, scrape one or two ends in an opposite radian with a bamboo knife to form a **harp crescent**.

CHAPTER THREE
Quilling of Adorable Zodiac Animals

*B*ased on the elements and basic techniques introduced in the previous chapter, the representative figures from the traditional Chinese zodiac form the theme of the works presented in this chapter, with twelve different characteristics to express their auspicious meanings. These twelve works are all simple pieces with beautiful colors, distinct traits, lively styles, and relatively simple composition, elements, and techniques that are suitable for equipping beginners with a basic idea of Chinese paper quilling.

On facing page

Fig. 16 *The Portrait of Lady*

The portrait of ladies is a type of traditional Chinese figure painting, depicting aristocratic women's lives as the subject. The earliest portraits of ladies can be traced back to the Warring States period (475–221 BC). At that time, portraits of ladies were mainly images of praying and flying to the sky, reflecting people's yearning for the unknown world. With the passing of time, the women depicted by painters have gradually changed from fairies and gods to idealized female images. In the Tang dynasty (618–907), portraits of ladies became mundane, and the women depicted were often plump, noble, and with casual demeanor, reflecting the aesthetic traits of the era of the prosperous Tang dynasty. In the Ming and Qing dynasties (1368–1911), portraits of ladies witnessed a new peak in its evolution. The women in the pictures were often elegant and refined, noble and ethereal, representing the artists' pursuit of pure aestheticism.

Drawing on the characteristics of Chinese figure painting, this work skillfully uses the texture of paper to shape the woman's body and clothes, making the lines smooth and round and the shape lifelike. The peony symbolizes wealth, auspiciousness, and completeness in Chinese culture. In the picture, the woman in blue holds up the folding fan as she dances. The peony blooms at the bottom of the picture match those on the folding fan, symbolizing good wishes for prosperity, well-being, and good fortune in life.

1. Mouse (for Affluence)

Mice have long been unpopular for their love of stealing food. However, if there are mice in the family, it indicates that the family is well off and has surplus food. So in the hearts of ancient Chinese people, a mouse symbolizes wealth.

In this work, the author uses the color of brown as the main tone and skillfully uses crescent elements to construct various parts of the mouse's body. With erect ears, a sharp mouth, a long tail, slender forelimbs, and strong hindlimbs, the artist captures the typical characteristics of a mouse and creates its alertness.

Colors and Elements

Back, bottom and tail	○ ○ ● ●	S crescent
Eye	● ● ○ ●	ring coil, transformed ring coil
Other parts of the rat	○ ○ ● ●	basic crescent
Flower	● ● ○	ring coil, transformed basic loop
Background	white watercolor paper (suggested size: 30 cm × 20 cm)	

1

Using rice white, light yellow, earthen yellow, ochre, and other color paper strips, make four basic crescents as shown in the picture, creating the head, mouth, and ears of the rat.

2

Make five basic crescents with rice white, light yellow, earthen yellow, and ochre strips as the hind leg, forelimbs, and chest of the rat.

3

Glue the starting ends of six strips in rice white, light yellow, earthen yellow, ochre, etc. in the way as making the basic crescent. After that, scrape them with a bamboo knife to produce radians.

4

Turn the strip over and continue to scrape the strip at the back end with a bamboo knife to make an S crescent.

5

Hold the head end of the strip with one hand and pull the strip out at different lengths with the other hand.

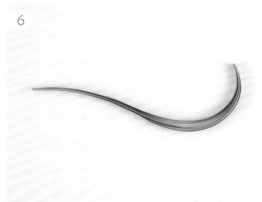

6

After gluing the tail end with glue, the excess part is cut and the S crescent shape of the rat's tail is completed. S crescent is a sort of warped basic crescent, and is a commonly used element in Chinese paper quilling.

7

Nine strips in the color of rice white, light yellow, earthen yellow, and ochre are used to make an S crescent, which serves as the back and bottom of the rat.

8

Make a basic loop with orange and ochre strips.

9

Gently squeeze the basic loop with your finger to warp it.

10

The transformed basic loop acts as a pattern component for the rat body. Make six identical pattern components.

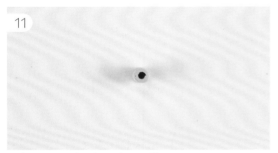

11

Make a ring coil with medium yellow strip.

12

Combine the ring coil with the transformed basic loop to form a flower as a pattern on the rat.

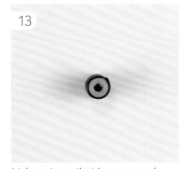

13

Make a ring coil with orange and black strips.

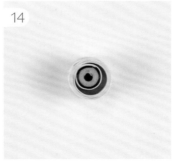

14

In addition to the first ring coil, add a light yellow ring coil.

15

Cover the ring coil with a layer of earthen yellow strip and pinch it with your thumb and forefinger.

16

The raindrop-like rat's eye is ready.

17

At the top left of the picture, lay out the rat's head and mouth.

18

Add ears to the rat's head.

19

Add the rat's back, bottom, and hind leg to the lower right side of the head.

20

Add the chest and limbs to the rat.

21

Add a tail to the rat.

22

Add the rat's eye.

23

Put a flower pattern on the rat's chest. Adjust the picture, fix it with glue, and the work is done.

2. Ox (for Diligence)

Ancient Chinese depended on farming for their livelihood, and cattle farming was an indispensable tool for agricultural development in ancient times. For this reason, Chinese people have always had affection for cattle and endowed them with such excellent qualities as hard work without expectation of rewards. In addition, in China, the bull is a symbol of momentum and strength, as in the "bull market" in securities.

In this work, the author uses many crescent elements to represent the shape of the bull. The curve of the crescent appropriately delineates the strength of the bull's muscles. The bull runs on all fours with tense muscles, angry eyes, and a strong momentum.

Colors and Elements

Body parts	○ ● ● ◡ ● ●	crescent
Nose	○ ◡ ● ● ● ●	hook crescent
Eye and ear	●	marquise coil, teardrop coil
Tail	● ●	curved line, marquise coil
Muscle lines	◡	curved line, broken line, long-tail scroll
Background	white watercolor paper (suggested size: 30 cm × 20 cm)	

Take light yellow, orange, earthen yellow, flesh color, ochre, burnt umber, and other colored paper strips to make three crescents as shown in the picture, forming the neck, back, and bottom of the ox.

Take light yellow, orange, earthen yellow, flesh color, ochre, burnt umber, and other colored paper strips to make two crescents, forming the chest and abdomen of the ox.

Take light yellow, orange, earthen yellow, flesh color, ochre, and burnt umber paper strips to form four crescents, making the limbs and horns of the ox.

Take light yellow, orange, earthen yellow, flesh color, ochre, and burnt umber paper strips to make a crescent.

Fold the crescent to form a hook.

This hook crescent is the nose of the ox.

Take the flesh color strips and make three curved and broken lines by scraping and folding, forming the muscle lines of the ox.

Take another flesh color strip and scrape it with a bamboo knife to make a radian.

Roll up the strip with slotted tool.

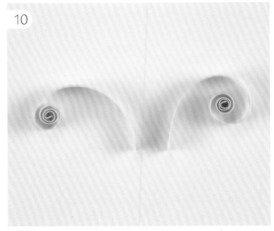

Cut the excess part of the strip and loosen it to form a long-tail scroll. Make two long, flesh color scrolls.

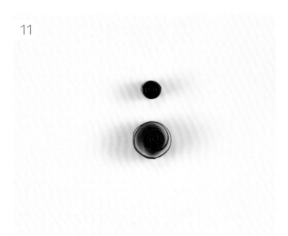

Make two loose coils with burnt umber strips.

Pinch the smaller loose coil with your thumb and forefinger at one end to form a teardrop coil.

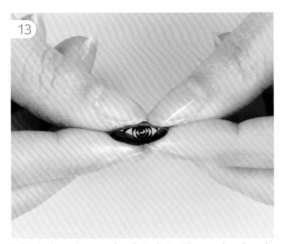

Take the large loose coil and pinch it with your thumb and forefinger at both ends to make a marquise coil.

Burnt umber teardrop coil and marquise coil are used as the ox's eye and ear.

15

Use burnt umber and earthen yellow strips to make a curved line and a marquise coil respectively as the tail of the ox.

16

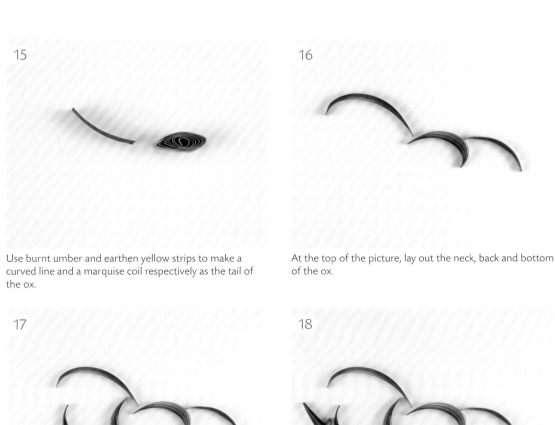

At the top of the picture, lay out the neck, back and bottom of the ox.

17

Then add the chest and abdomen of the ox.

18

Add limbs and nose to the ox.

19

Add horns, ear and eye to the ox.

20

Add flesh color muscle lines to the bull. Adjust the picture, fix it with glue, and the work is done.

3. Tiger (for Magnificence)

The tiger is mighty and masculine, and known as the king of beasts. In ancient China, the image of the tiger was highly worshipped, especially in the military field. The military signs used to dispatch soldiers were called "tiger charms," and those who fought bravely and invincibly were called "tiger generals." In addition, the tiger was also considered the guardian god of children, so parents would dress their children with tiger caps and shoes.

In this work, the author uses orange and black as the main colors for the tiger, using the basic crescent and S crescent to show the markings of the tiger. Although the tiger is resting on its stomach, its bronze-bell-like eyes, and the large character of "王(king)" on its forehead shows its inviolable majesty.

Colors and Elements

Body and tail	●	curved line
Limbs	●	basic crescent
Patterns on the chest, face, body and limbs	●	crescent, S crescent
Patterns on the tail	●	crescent coil
Head and nose	●	hook crescent
Nose tip	●	crescent coil
Eyes	○ ● ●	tight scroll, marquise coil
Mouth	●	curved line
Ears	●	basic crescent
The character of "王 (king)"	●	leaf coil
Background		white watercolor paper (suggested size: 30 cm × 20 cm)

1

Use orange strips to make curved lines as shown in the picture for the tiger's body and tail.

2

Take orange strips and make three basic crescents for the tiger's limbs.

3

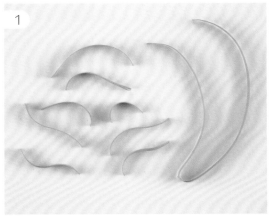

Take black strips and make five S crescents as the patterns on the body.

4

Use black strips to make a number of crescents as shown in the picture to form another pattern.

5

Take black strip and make a loose coil.

6

Press one side of the loose coil to the other side with the forefinger and thumb of both hands to form a crescent shape.

7

Make eight crescent coils with black strips as the patterns for the tiger's tail and the nose tip.

8

Take the orange strip and make two hook crescents as shown in the picture for the tiger's head.

9

Use orange strip to make a hook crescent-shaped tiger nose.

10

Make tight coils with light yellow and black strips and put them into burnt umber marquise coils to form the tiger's eyes. Then make three curved lines with red strips for the mouth of the tiger.

11

Use black strips to make two basic crescents as the tiger's ears. Then make three loose coils with red strips and flatten them into leaf coils as the character for "王 (king)" on the tiger's forehead.

12

On the top left of the background, add the tiger's head. Under the head, add four orange curved lines as the tiger's chest.

13

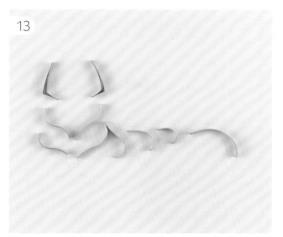

Continue to add orange curved lines to make up the tiger's body.

14

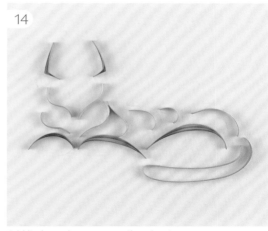

Add limbs and an orange tail to the tiger.

15

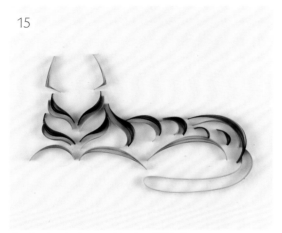

On the tiger's chest and body, add black crescent patterns.

16

Under the tiger's limbs, add four black crescents as patterns on the tiger's limbs.

17

Add two ears and the character "王 (king)" to the tiger's forehead. Add the eyes, nose, nose tip, and mouth to the tiger's head.

18

Add black crescent patterns to the tiger's face. Add black crescent coils as patterns on its tail. Adjust the picture, fix it with glue, and the work is done.

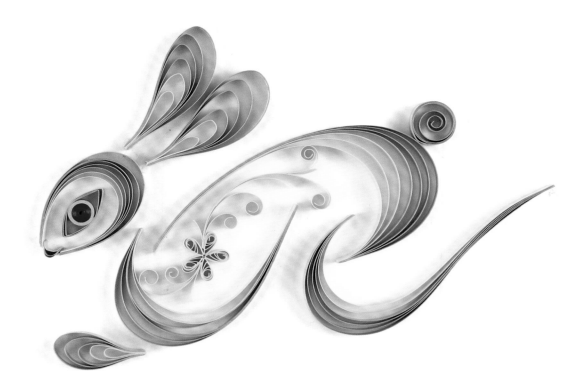

4. Rabbit (for Smartness)

Rabbits are smart, adorable, gentle, and kind. They are deeply loved by Chinese people and are regarded as auspicious omens. In Chinese mythology, there is a rabbit named Jade Rabbit, which makes elixirs in the Moon Palace. People have connected the rabbit with the moon since ancient times, and the rabbit has come to be the symbol of the moon.

In this work, the author uses gray and light green as the main tones of the rabbit, showing the cleverness and flexibility of the rabbit in the shape of the crescent. Long ears and red eye highlight the main characteristics of the rabbit. The decorative patterns on its body makes the rabbit more artistic and aesthetic.

Colors and Elements

Ears and forelimb	○ ●	transformed basic loop
Head, mouth, chest, back, and hindlimb	○ ●	basic crescent
Tail	●	loose coil
Eye	● ● ●	tight coil, marquise coil
Patterns on body	○	teardrop coil, curved line, long-tail scroll
Background		white watercolor paper (suggested size: 30 cm × 20 cm)

1

Make a basic loop with light green and medium gray strips.

2

Pinch one end of the basic loop.

3

Make an irregular warp of the basic loop.

4

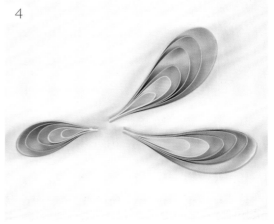

Make two big and one small transformed basic loops for the ears and forelimb of the rabbit.

5

Make five basic crescents with light green and medium gray strips for the rabbit's head, mouth, chest, back, and hindlimb.

6

Make a loose coil with medium gray strip for the rabbit's tail.

7

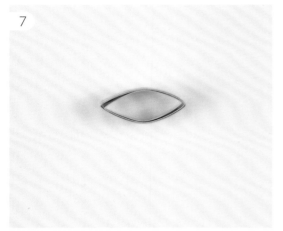

Make a marquise coil with medium gray strips for the rabbit's eye.

8

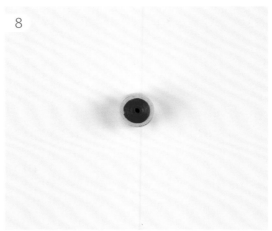

Make a tight coil with deep red and pink strips as the pupil of the eye.

9

Put the tight coil into the marquise coil, and the rabbit's eye is finished.

10

Use light green strips to make five teardrop coils.

11

Make a flower out of the teardrop coils.

12

Use light green strips to make some curved lines and long-tail scrolls.

13

Combine these curved lines with the long-tail scrolls and the flower to form the patterns on the rabbit.

14

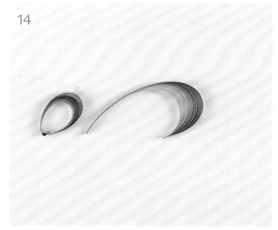

Add the rabbit's head, mouth, and back to the background paper.

15

Add the rabbit's chest and hindlimb.

16

Add the eye and tail to the rabbit.

17

Add the rabbit's ears.

18

Put patterns on the rabbit. Adjust the picture, fix it with glue, and the work is done.

5. Dragon (for Power)

The dragon is a legendary animal in China, symbolizing auspiciousness and ancient imperial power. In legend, the dragon's horns resemble a deer's, its head resembles an ox's, its eyes resemble a shrimp's, its mouth resembles a donkey's, its belly resembles a snake's, its scales resemble a fish's, its feet resemble a phoenix's, its beard resembles a human's, and its ears resemble an elephant's. It can fly the highest of heavens and swim the deepest of waters. Divine and inviolable, it can summon the wind and command the rain. The dragon is the most representative cultural totem of the Chinese nation, leaving an endless legacy in the long river of history and legend.

In this work, the author uses blue as the main color of the dragon, with brown claws, red pupils, flying beard and hair. Under the dragon are two auspicious clouds, symbolizing that it flies in the heavens, majestic and regal.

Colors and Elements

Body and head	●	basic crescent
Tail	●	basic loop
Horns, beard and hair	●	curved leaf loop
Claws	●	curved raindrop loop
Eye and antennae	● ○ ●	loose coil, curved line
Clouds	● ● ●	transformed crescent, transformed loop
Background	white watercolor paper (suggested size: 30 cm × 20 cm)	

1

Take the cobalt blue strips and make five basic crescents for the body and head of the dragon.

2

Make six basic loops with cobalt blue strips for the dragon's tail.

3

Make a basic loop with a cobalt blue strip.

4

Pinch and bend the basic loop with both hands.

5

The basic loop is transformed into a curved leaf loop as the dragon's horn.

6

Use cobalt blue strips to make a number of curved leaf loops of different lengths, which are used as the dragon's horns, beard, and hair.

7

Make several basic loops with burnt umber strips, then bend and pinch them into curved raindrop loops for the dragon's claws.

8

9

Make loose coils with deep red and white strips as the dragon's eye. Two S shaped curved lines are made with pink strips for the antennae of the dragon.

Make a basic crescent with pink purple, pink green, and sky blue strips.

10

11

Don't trim the strips, but fold it backwards at the end of the crescent.

After the first crescent, continue to make the second continuous crescent.

12

13

At the end of the second crescent, fold the strips backwards and make a third continuous crescent.

Scrape the third crescent into an S crescent with a bamboo knife, and glue the end of the S crescent to the beginning of the first crescent to form an auspicious cloud.

14

15

Make a basic loop with pink purple, pink green, and sky blue strips.

Scrape the end of this basic loop out of the radian with a bamboo knife.

16

Pinch the other end of the basic loop with your thumb and forefinger.

17

The second auspicious cloud is completed.

18

On the background paper, lay out the dragon's head and body.

19

Add the dragon's hair and horns.

20

Add the dragon's eye and antennae to the head. Add the tail at the end of the dragon body.

21

Put the dragon's claws in the appropriate places. Under the dragon, overlay two auspicious clouds. Adjust the picture, fix it with glue, and the work is done.

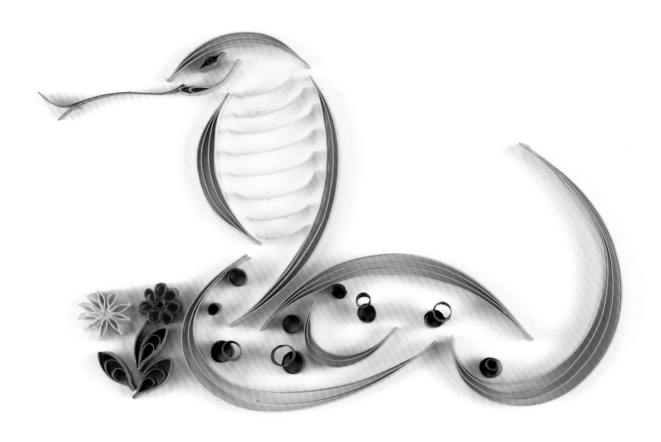

6. Snake (for Agility)

The snake is one of the important totems of the Chinese people. According to ancient Chinese mythology and legends, Nüwa, the goddess who created human and repaired the leaking sky, and Fuxi, the inventor of the Eight Diagrams and the Characters, are both images with the head of a human being and the body of a snake.

In this work, the author uses grass green as the main color to shape the image of snake, and several concise crescents outline its shape. Two small flowers, one red and one yellow, as well as the green leaves, show the snake's living environment. The snake holds its head high and sticks out its tongue, looking fierce and lifelike.

Colors and Elements

Body	●	basic crescent
Chest texture	○	curved line
Eye	●●	ring coil, marquise coil
Mouth	●	curved leaf loop
Tongue	●	curved line
Red flower	●	ring coil
Yellow flower	○	leaf coil
Leaf blade 1	●	leaf loop
Leaf blade 2	●	loose coil
Background		white watercolor paper (suggested size: 30 cm × 20 cm)

1

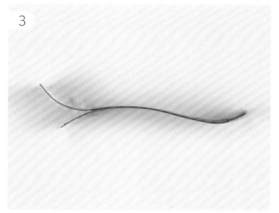

Use grass green strips to make seven basic crescents of different sizes for the snake's body.

2

Take the light green strips and make several curved lines for the texture of the snake's chest. Take ultramarine blue and grass green strips, make the snake's eye using the same method for making the rabbit's eye (see page 44). Then make a curved leaf loop with grass green strip to form the mouth of the snake.

3

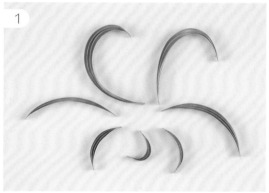

Take red strips and make two curved lines to piece together the snake's tongue.

4

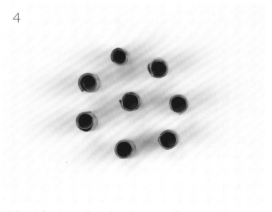

Make eight ring coils with red strips as flower petals.

5

Put these eight ring coils together to form a flower.

6

Make ten leaf coils with lemon yellow strips.

7

Put ten leaf coils together to form a yellow flower.

8

Make three leaf loops with dark green strips for the leaves of flowers.

9

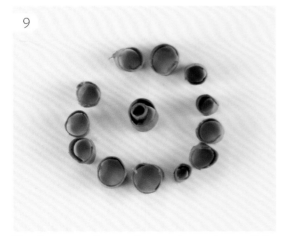

Use olive green strips to make more than ten loose coils for another type of leaves.

10

On the background paper, lay out the upper half of the snake's body.

11

Continue to add crescents for the snake's body.

12

Add the lower part of the snake's body and the tail.

13

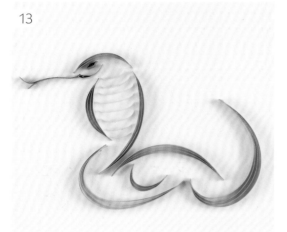

Add the snake's mouth, eye, and tongue, as well as the chest texture.

14

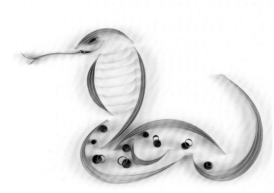

Add olive green leaves to the snake body.

15

On the left side of the snake, add two flowers.

16

Add dark green leaves to the bottom of the flower. Adjust the picture, fix it with glue, and the work is done.

7. Horse (for Speed)

The horse can gallop thousands of miles, as fast as the wind. It was not only an important means of transportation in ancient China, but also a powerful beast for military use. Ancient Chinese emperors and generals were always proud of their horses. In addition, a horse is also a symbol of the national spirit that the Chinese nation has advocated since ancient times, which is called "the vigorous spirit of dragon and horse."

In this work, the artist uses orange and deep red strips to create a speeding chestnut horse. The use of crescent elements skillfully shows the muscular lines of the horse. The S crescents of the mane and the tail waving upward creates a sense of swift movement when the horse is running at full speed.

Colors and Elements

Body and hindlimbs		crescent
Head		hook crescent, S crescent
Mane		S crescent
Forelimbs		leaf coil
Eye and ears		marquise coil
Horsetail		combination of curved lines
Butterflies		tight coil, teardrop coil
Grass		basic crescent
Background		white watercolor paper (suggested size: 30 cm × 20 cm)

1

Use orange and deep red strips to make the crescents as shown in the picture for the horse's body and hindlimbs.

2

Use orange and deep red strips to make four S crescents for the horse mane. Then make a hook crescent and an S crescent for the horse head.

3

Take orange strips and make four leaf coils for the horse's fore limbs.

4

Make marquise coils with black strips to form the horse's eye. Then use orange strips to make the ears, one of which can be pinched asymmetrically, so there is variation in the marquise coils.

5

Take orange and deep red strips, cut them short, and glue them together at one end.

6

Use a bamboo knife to scrape them in one direction.

7

When the strip produces a radian, it becomes the tail of the horse, waving upward.

8

Make four ultramarine blue tight coils and four light blue teardrop coils.

9

Make two long basic crescents with olive green strips for grass.

10

At the top left of the background, lay out the horse's head and neck.

11

Continue to add crescents to form the horse body.

12

Add forelimbs and hindlimbs to the horse.

13

Arrange the S crescent mane evenly on the horse's neck. Put a raised tail on the horse's rump.

14

Continue to add the horse's eye and ears.

15

Add green grass to the ground.

16

By the front and rear legs of the horse, piece two butterflies together, which are startled by the fleet horse. Adjust the picture, fix it with glue, and the work is done.

8. Goat (for Kindness)

The goat is kind and gentle, and loved by people. In ancient China, goat was a symbol of beauty. The character for "beauty" in Chinese was composed of the character for "goat" and the character for "big." People often used the phrase "a lamb kneeling for milk" to teach children to be grateful and filial, and the phrase "three rams bring bliss" to imply good luck and peace.

In this work, the artist uses light green and sky blue as the main colors, and uses crescents to show a woolly texture. With two horns on the head and a long beard under the jaw, the charmingly naive goat leaps from the paper.

Colors and Elements

Body parts		basic crescent, S crescent
Four limbs		leaf coil
Horns and ear		curved teardrop coil
Wool		basic crescent
Eye		tight coil, marquise coil
Grass		teardrop coil
Background	white watercolor paper (suggested size: 30 cm × 20 cm)	

1

Take the sky blue strips and make basic crescents and S crescents as shown in the picture, forming the goat's body parts.

2

Take the sky blue strips and make four leaf coils for the four limbs of the goat.

3

Use sky blue and khaki strips to make the horns and ear of goat.

4

Use light green strips to make five basic crescents for the wool.

5

The two ends of a basic crescent can be bound to form a new element.

6

Make the goat's eye out of medium gray strips.

7

Make eight teardrop coils with light green strips for grass.

8

On the right side of the background, lay out the head and mouth of the goat.

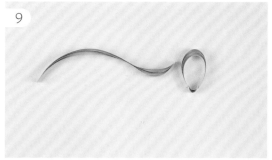

9

On the left side of the goat's head, add an S crescent as its back.

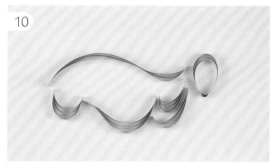

10

Under the back of the goat, add the abdomen.

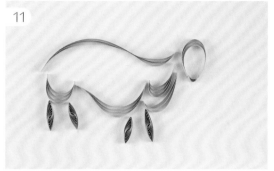

11

Under the abdomen, add four limbs.

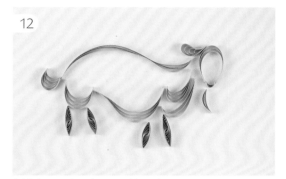

12

Add the goat's tail, ear, and beard.

13

Add the eye to the head of the goat.

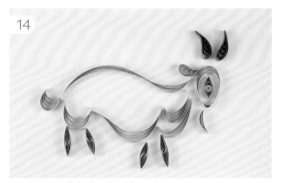

14

On the top of the head, add two horns.

15

Add wool to the goat.

16

On the ground, make three groups of green grass. Adjust the picture, fix it with glue, and the work is done.

9. Monkey (for Well-Being)

Monkeys are agile and clever. In China, the most popular image of a monkey is the Monkey King, who caused havoc in the Temple of Heaven in *Journey to the West*. Among the twelve zodiac signs, monkey ranks ninth, representing longevity, while peaches are also symbol of longevity, so the image of a monkey offering peach implies a long life. In addition, the Chinese character for "monkey" is also homophonic with the character meaning "noble" or "high official," so the monkey also implies a promotion.

In this work, the author uses the auspicious implication of a monkey offering a peach as a token of longevity. With a couple of simple elements, it outlines the shape of the monkey, vivid and impressive. The huge pink peach in the monkey's hand is the visual focus of the whole work, embodying the artist's wishes for longevity and well-being.

Colors and Elements

Head and ear	○ ●	basic crescent
Upper part of leg, right arm	●	hook crescent
Left arm	●	marquise coil
Back, lower part of leg	●	basic crescent
Paws	●	basic crescent, curved raindrop loop
Tail	●	combination of curved lines
Eye	● ○ ◉	tight coil
Peach	◉ ○	basic crescent
Peach leaves	○	basic crescent
Background		white watercolor paper (suggested size: 30 cm × 20 cm)

1

Make a basic crescent with lemon yellow and burnt umber strips for the monkey's head.

2

Make two basic crescents with lemon yellow strips for the monkey's face, and make a basic crescent with burnt umber strips for its ear.

3

Make two hook crescents with burnt umber strips for the upper half of the monkey's leg and the right arm.

4

Make a marquise coil with burnt umber strip to form the left arm of the monkey.

5

Make three basic crescents with burnt umber strips for the back and the lower half of the leg.

6

Make three burnt umber basic crescents for the monkey's paws.

7

Using the techniques of pinching and bending, process three burnt umber basic loops into curved raindrop loops as another form of the monkey's paws.

8

Take two burnt umber strips and fold them in half together.

9

Scrape these two strips with a bamboo knife to make a radian.

10

Pull out some of the paper from inside to create some space between the two strips to form the monkey's tail.

11

Make tight coils with black, lemon yellow, and orange strips for the monkey's eye.

12

Make two crescents with pink and light pink strips to form the peach. Then make three crescent-shaped peach leaves with light green strips.

13

At the top of the background, lay out the monkey's head and face.

14

Add the monkey's back and lower part of the leg under the head.

15

Add the monkey's arms and the upper half of the leg.

16

On the top of the monkey's leg, add the left forepaw of the monkey, using curved raindrop loops.

17

Add a crescent-shaped right forepaw and hind paw to the monkey.

18

Add the monkey's tail.

19

Add the eye and the ear to the face.

20

On the monkey's right forepaw, assemble a pink peach.

21

Under the peach, add three leaves. Adjust the picture, fix it with glue, and the work is done.

10. Rooster (for Virtue)

The character for "rooster" and the character for "auspicious" are homophones in Chinese, making it an auspicious symbol. In ancient China, rooster was believed to have five virtues: literary, military, courage, benevolence, and trustworthiness. The rooster is the prototype of the phoenix, a divine bird in traditional Chinese culture. It is also a symbol of light, order, and diligence as it crows early in the morning day after day. It fights bravely and never fails, so people also use it to symbolize exorcism and refuge, regarding it as a door god.

In this work, the author decorates the rooster with colorful feathers to make it look gorgeous. Its head is high, its crown bright red, and it is self-confident, as if it were greeting the arrival of light with its call.

Colors and Elements

Feathers	● ● ● ○ ● ●	crescent
Wing	○ ●	marquise coil, hook crescent
Crown, fleshy skin	●	curved teardrop coil, marquise coil, S crescent, basic crescent
Claws, beak	●	basic crescent, hook crescent
Eye	● ◖ ●	tight coil
Background	white watercolor paper (suggested size: 30 cm × 20 cm)	

1

Make two basic crescents with red strips for the feathers on the rooster's neck.

2

Take jade green and grass green strips to make two crescents as the feathers on the rooster's body.

3

Use ultramarine blue and Prussian blue strips to make four crescents as the feathers on the rooster's tail.

4

Make three basic crescents with medium yellow strips for more feathers.

5

Take sky blue strips and make three hook crescents for the feathers at the end of the wing.

6

Make three marquise coils with medium yellow strips to form the feathers on the top of the wing.

7

Make basic crescent, S crescent, marquise coil, and curved teardrop coil with red strips as the rooster's crown and fleshy skin.

8

Make basic crescents and hook crescents with khaki strips for the beak and claws of the rooster.

9

Use black, lemon yellow, and orange strips to make a tight coil for the eye of the rooster.

10

On the background paper, piece together the rooster's neck with red feathers.

11

Use green feathers to make the rooster's body.

12

Make the rooster's tail with blue feathers.

13

Add eye and beak above the rooster's neck.

14

Add the crown and fleshy skin around the eye and beak. Add sky blue feathers at the end of the wing.

15

Add the medium yellow crescent-shaped feathers to the neck and the abdomen. At the top of the wing, add medium yellow marquise coil-shaped feathers.

16

Add the rooster's claws to the bottom of its body. Adjust the picture, fix it with glue, and the work is done.

11. Dog (for Prosperity)

Dogs are the most loyal friends of humans. They are friendly and pleasant. The homophone of the dog's bark, "wang," and the Chinese character "wang (旺)" suggesting prosperity have led the dog to be endowed with the meaning of "wealth or fortune."

   In this work, the artist chooses the crescent elements to form the shape of the dog, ingeniously simulating the texture of the dog's fluffy fur. The dog sticks out its long tongue, opens its big eyes, and looks at the bone in front of its chest. It's very cute and lovable.

Colors and Elements

Body parts	● ●	crescent
Fur around the eyes	○	transformed loose coil
Eyes	● ○ ●	tight coil
Nose	●	transformed coil
Skull	●	basic crescent
Tongue	●	marquise coil
Bone	●	combination of scrolls
Background	white watercolor paper (suggested size: 30 cm × 20 cm)	

1

Use orange strips to form crescents for all parts of the dog's body.

2

Make a loose coil with medium yellow strips.

3

At the point where all the multi-layer strips in the loose coil are overlapped, paste them together.

4

Then paste the inner loops on the opposite side of the first sticking point to form a pumpkin shape.

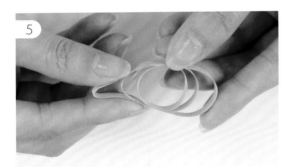

5

Bend and pinch this element.

6

Make two such elements for the fur around the dog's eyes.

7

Make two tight coils with black, lemon yellow, and orange strips for the dog's eyes.

8

Take a piece of medium gray strip and roll up its two ends with a slotted tool.

9

Make two medium gray double-headed rolls.

10

Paste the middle point of the two double-headed rolls to form a bone.

11

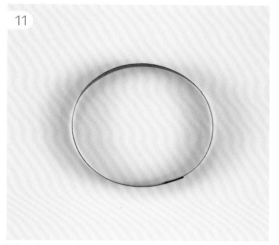

Take a burnt umber strip to make a coil.

12

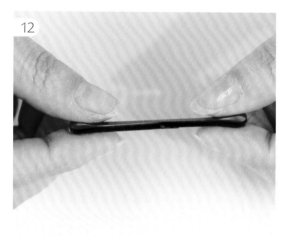

Knead the paper coil flat and turn it into a double-layered strip.

13

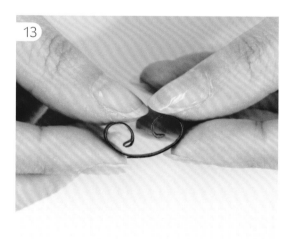

Roll up the two ends of this strip.

14

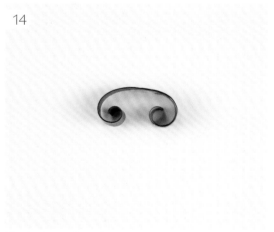

The dog's nose is ready.

15

Make a crescent-shaped dog's skull with burnt umber strip and a marquise coil with red strip as the dog's tongue.

16

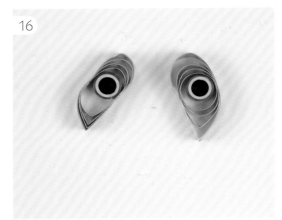

In the upper left of the background, add the fur around the dog's eyes, and then put the two eyes into them.

17

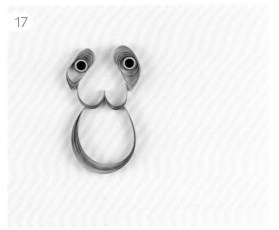

Use the crescents to lay out the dog's jaw and chest.

18

Lay out the dog's limbs and rump.

19

Add the ears and tail to the dog.

20

Finally, add the skull, nose, tongue and bone. Adjust the picture, fix it with glue, and the work is done.

12. Pig (for Blessing)

The Chinese people began to intentionally domesticate and raise pigs as early as the Neolithic Age, eight or nine thousand years ago. In the tombs of ancient people, there are often pig remains, which indicates the status and richness of the tomb owner. The pig's plump ears are regarded as a symbol of blessing. The lower part of the Chinese character for "family" actually means "pig." It can be seen that the ancients felt that the pig was a symbol of wealth in the family.

In this work, the author uses pink as the main color, with a purple flower-like pattern, to vividly show a naive piglet. Piglets are round and full in shape, giving people a sense of abundance and happiness.

Colors and Elements

Body parts	●	crescent
Eye and nostril	●	marquise coil
Hooves	●	marquise coil
Bristles	●	crescent
Patterns	○ ● ●	loose coil, teardrop coil
Background	white watercolor paper (suggested size: 30 cm × 20 cm)	

1

Use pink strips to make the crescents as shown in the picture, forming all parts of the pig.

2

Make six marquise coils with black strips and pink strips for the pig's eye, nostril, and hooves.

3

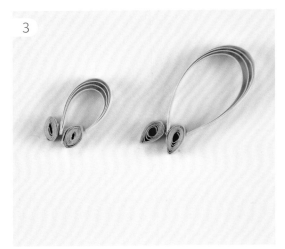

Paste pink marquise coils onto the crescents for the limbs.

4

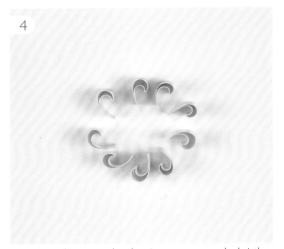

Take the pink strips and make nine crescents as the bristles.

5

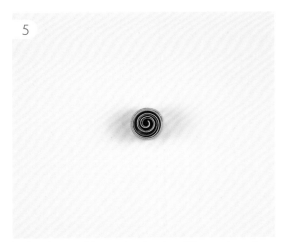

Make a loose coil by overlapping the white, purple, and light purple strips.

6

Make twelve teardrop coils with white, purple, and light purple strips.

7

Taking the loose coil as the center, put the teardrop coils together to form the pattern on the pig.

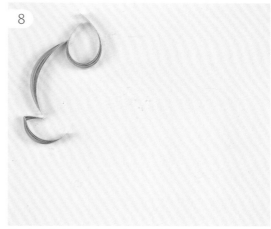

8

On the left side of the background, lay out the pig's forehead, nose, and ear.

9

Continue to lay out the pig's back, abdomen, and tail.

10

Add the limbs to the pig.

11

Arrange the bristles neatly on the pig's forehead.

12

Add purple pattern to the pig. Adjust the picture, fix it with glue, and the work is done.

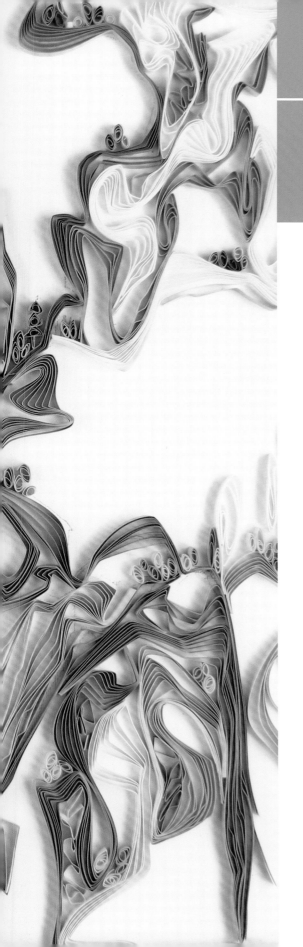

CHAPTER FOUR
Quilling of Lucky Animals

*F*ollowing the production of paper quillings of the figures in the Chinese zodiac presented in the previous chapter, this chapter will continue with our creative journey. Compared with the twelve zodiac series, the composition, elements, and techniques of the works presented in this chapter are more complex and varied, while the auspicious meanings presented are equally rich and compact. You can give full play to your imagination and creativity in your study, producing fascinating, ingenious paper quilling works of your own.

Fig. 17 *Landscape Series* (Picture Four)
See page 4 for details.

1. Duck (for Honor)

The imperial examinations of the Ming (1368–1644) and Qing (1644–1911) dynasties in China were divided into four grades, the last one being the Palace Examination, which was conducted by the emperor in person. The candidates admitted to the Palace Examination were divided into three grades. The first place in the first grade was the champion. It was the highest honor that ancient Chinese scholars yearned for. In traditional Chinese culture, there is a character "甲" meaning "top" in the character "duck (鸭)," so a duck is often used to imply "the top one."

In this work, the artist uses a large number of crescents and warped crescents to represent the image of duck. The yellow duckling, swimming on the blue water, appears relaxed and adorable, and carries the author's best wishes.

Colors and Elements

Waves	○ ○ ● ●	basic crescent, wave crescent
Duck body parts	○ ○ ●	combination of curved lines, crescent
Feathers	○ ●	basic crescent, wave crescent
Beak	●	hook crescent
Eye	○ ●	tight coil
Background	white watercolor paper (suggested size: 30 cm × 20 cm)	

1

Take blue strips and make more than a dozen basic crescents for the waves.

2

Make another five basic crescents with blue strips, then roll their heads and transform them into wave crescents.

3

Use light yellow, lemon yellow and orange strips to make the parts of the duck's body as shown in the picture. Refer to the tail of the project *Monkey* (see page 62) for the making of the duck's head.

4

Take dark green and light yellow strips to make nine basic crescents for the feathers on the duck wings.

5

Make two wave crescents and one hook crescent with dark green strips for feathers on neck and the duck beak.

6

Make a tight coil with black strips and white strips, and then pinch it to make an oval shape for the eye of duck.

7

On the background, put together the head, neck, and back of the duck.

8

Add the duck's beak and eye to its head.

9

Add feathers at the end of the wing near the duck's tail.

10

Continue to add feathers at the beginning of the wing.

11

Add dark green wave crescent feathers to the neck of the duck.

12

Continue to add light yellow and dark green feathers to the wing.

13

Under the duck, add the crescent-shaped blue waves.

14

Continue to add wave crescent-shaped waves. Adjust the picture, fix it with glue, and the work is done.

2. Panda (for Treasure)

The giant panda, a creature unique to China and known as its "national treasure," is an endangered animal mainly inhabiting Sichuan Province. Its main characteristics include its black and white fur, its love of bamboo, its adorable shape, its clumsy movements, and its docile temperament. All these traits make it a favorite of people.

In this work, the author ingeniously uses the crescent elements to construct the panda's body and limbs, creating a vivid image of a giant panda playing on the grass.

Colors and Elements

Head and body	●	crescent
Eyes, ears and nose	●	transformed ring coil
Limbs	●	basic crescent
Grass	● ● ●	loose coil, teardrop coil
Background	white watercolor paper (suggested size: 30 cm × 20 cm)	

1

Use purple strips to make the crescent elements as shown in the picture to create the head and body of the panda.

2

Make five ring coils with black strips, and then use the pinching technique to transform them into the panda's eyes, ears, and nose.

3

Make five basic crescents with black strips for the panda's limbs.

4

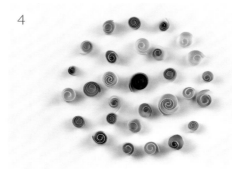

Using blue and green paper strips, make many loose coils for grass.

5

Use blue and green strips to make six teardrop coils.

6

Piece together the panda's head at the top of the background paper.

7

Put the body of the panda to the lower left of its head.

8

Add eyes to the panda's face.

9

Continue to add the panda's ears and nose.

10

Use black crescents to make the panda's upper limbs.

11

Add the panda's lower limbs.

12

Add the loose coils under the panda's body as grass.

13

Place some grass on the body of the panda.

14

Finally, add some teardrop coil grass. Adjust the picture, fix it with glue, and the work is complete.

3. Peacock (for Beauty)

The peacock is a beautiful ornamental bird, known as the "king of birds," which symbolizes auspiciousness, kindness, beauty, and luxury. The peacock's spreading tail actually indicates what a male peacock does when it is courting, continually making various elegant movements to show off its beauty to the female peacock. In traditional Chinese culture, the peacock's spreading tail symbolizes great fortune.

In this work, the author uses simple elements, elegant colors and exquisite composition to vividly show the pride, beauty, and luxury of a male peacock that is courting a mate with its spreading tail.

Colors and Elements

Neck and body	● ○	crescent
Wings	●	wave crescent
Wing feathers	○	curved leaf loop
Head	● ○	leaf coil
Head feathers	● ●	combination of curved lines, ring coil
Tail feathers	○ ●	raindrop loop, combination of curved lines
Background		white watercolor paper (suggested size: 30 cm × 20 cm)

1

2

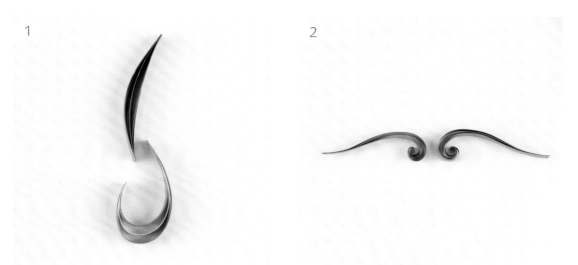

Make two crescents with jade green and lemon yellow strips for the peacock's neck and body.

Make two wave crescents with jade green strips for the peacock's wings.

3

4

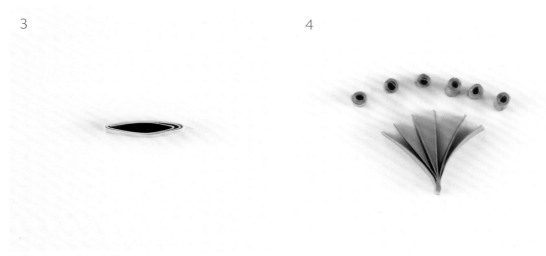

Make a loose coil with black and lemon yellow strips and flatten it into a leaf coil for the head of the peacock.

Use jade green and red strips to make the curved line combination and ring coils, forming the peacock's head feathers.

5

Make six curved leaf loops with lemon yellow strips for the feathers of the peacock's wings.

6

Make a dozen raindrop loops with jade green and lemon yellow strips for the feathers on the peacock's tail.

7

Use jade green and lemon yellow strips to make several sets of combination of curved lines, forming feathers at the end of the tail.

8

In the middle of the background paper, lay out the peacock's neck and body.

9

Add the head on the peacock's neck.

10

Add the feathers on the peacock's head.

11

Complete the head feathers with ring coils.

12

Add its wings on both sides of the body.

13

Add lemon yellow feathers to the wings.

14

Around the peacock's head, add raindrop loops as the tail feathers.

15

Continue to add the tail feathers.

16

Finally, add more feathers at the end of the tail feathers. Adjust the picture, fix it with glue, and the work is done.

4. Heron (for Success)

This works presents traditional auspicious patterns to wish candidates a smooth imperial examination, which was very popular in the Qing dynasty. Characters of "heron" and "road" are homophonic, while "lotus" and "continuous" are homophonic, so an egret and a pool of lotus together implies the wish for continuous ascent.

In this work, the artist depicts the scene of an egret preying on fish in a lotus pond through ingenious composition, elegant colors and skilled techniques. The whole picture is both dynamic and static, simple and elegant.

Colors and Elements

Egret body parts	●	crescent, curved leaf loop
Egret tail	●	combination of curved lines
Egret feet	●	broken line
Fish	●	curved line, broken line
Egret eye, fish eye	● ○	tight coil
Water	●	curved line
Lotus leaf frames	● ●	transformed coil
Stem and lotus leaf veins	● ●	curved line, loose coil, combination of loops
Lotus flower	● ●	teardrop coil, crescent
Background		white watercolor paper (suggested size: 30 cm × 20 cm)

1

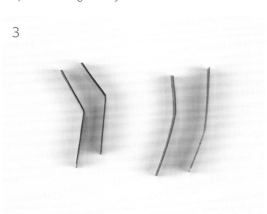

Make curved leaf loops and crescents with sky blue strips, for parts of the egret body.

2

Use sky blue strip to make a combination of curved lines for the egret's tail.

3

Use dark gray strips to make broken lines for the egret's feet.

4

Use red strips to make a broken line and two curved lines for fish.

5

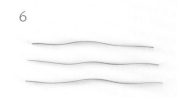

6

7

Make two tight coils with black and lemon yellow strips for the eyes of egret and fish. The egret's eye is flattened to form an oval shape.

Use ultramarine blue strips to make curved waves.

Make two large loose coils with mint green and grass green strips, then use the techniques of scraping, bending, and pinching to form the border of two lotus leaves.

8

9

Make the stem and leaf veins of the first lotus flower with grass green strips.

Take the mint green strip and bend the starting end into a loop.

10

11

Bend out three loops in succession, then put the rest of the strip around the three loops.

Paste and fix the outermost loop, and cut out the excess paper to form a combination of loops. Make six sets of combination of loops with mint green strips.

12

13

Use rose red and pink strips to make a teardrop coil and six crescents as lotus petals. Put these seven petals together to form a complete lotus flower.

On the left side of the background paper, lay out the head, neck, and beak of the egret.

14

On the right side of the egret's head, continue to piece out the egret's body. Add the wing and legs to its body.

15

Add the tail, feet and eye to the egret.

16

At the beak of the egret, make the red fish. Add the waves to the feet of the egret.

17

On the right side of the egret, add the frames of two lotus leaves and a lotus stem.

18

Inside the lower lotus leaf, add the loop combinations to form the vein of the leaves. In the upper lotus leaf, add curved lines and loose coil to form the vein of the leaves.

19

Add the lotus flower to the lotus stem. Adjust the picture, fix it with glue, and the work is done.

5. Cat and Butterfly (for Wellness)

Mao die refers to the age of eighty or ninety. "Cat" is a homophone of *mao* and "butterfly" is a homophone of *die*. The picture of a cat and a butterfly playing together implies an old man's longevity.

In this work, the author uses very concise elements to depict a lively, adorable kitten and a flying butterfly. The whole picture is bright in color, well-designed in composition, sophisticated in technique, relaxed and lively in atmosphere, embodying the author's good wishes for the elderly to live a long life.

Colors and Elements

Cat body parts	●	combination of curved lines
Head and paws	●	crescent
Nose and mouth	●	crescent coil
Eyes	● ●	loose coil, marquise coil
Butterfly wings	● ●	combination of loops
Butterfly body	◡	leaf loop
Butterfly antennae	●	long-tail scroll
Background	white watercolor paper (suggested size: 30 cm × 20 cm)	

1

Take the rose red strips and make the cat's body parts in the same way as making horse's tail (see page 55) in the project *Horse*.

2

Take the rose red strips and make six crescents for cat's head and paws.

3

Shape light brown loose coils and medium gray marquise coils to make the cat's eyes, and make rose red crescent coils for the cat's nose and mouth.

4

Use sky blue and cobalt blue strips to make two sets of combination of loops for the wings of the butterfly.

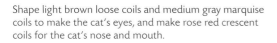

5

Make a leaf loop with light yellow strip as the butterfly's body, and make two long-tail scrolls with cobalt blue strips for the butterfly's antennae.

6

On the left side of the background paper, lay out the cat's head with two rose red crescents.

7

Add the ears and whiskers to the cat's face.

8

On the right side of the cat's head, add the cat's body and limbs.

9

Add the cat's tail and the claws at the end of each limb.

10

Add the eyes, nose and mouth to the cat's head.

11

Above the cat, lay out the butterfly. Adjust the picture, fix it with glue, and the work is done.

6. Tortoise (for Longevity)

The Chinese regard tortoises as spiritual animals. Xuan Wu, one of the four spirits of heaven, is the image of half tortoise and half snake. The oldest and mature oracle bone inscription in China is also engraved on tortoise shells. A tortoise has a very long life, making it a symbol of longevity.

In this work, the artist captures the main characteristics of the tortoise, and uses polygonal paper coils to show the patterns of the tortoise shell. A small tortoise is added to the back of the big one, making the whole work lovely and intersting.

Colors and Elements

Big tortoise body parts	●	crescent, combination of loops
Shell	● ○	polygon coil
Shell edge	●	crescent, square coil
Claws	●	combination of curved lines, curved leaf loop
Small tortoise	○ ●	crescent coil, curved line, curved leaf loop
Tortoises' eyes	●	tight coil
Background	white watercolor paper (suggested size: 30 cm × 20 cm)	

| 1 | 2 | 3 |

Use light brown strips to make the parts of the tortoise's body as shown in the picture.

Form a crescent shape with jade green strips as the boundary between the shell and the edge of the shell.

Make ten jade green square coils by using the technique for making quadrilateral coils.

| 4 | 5 |

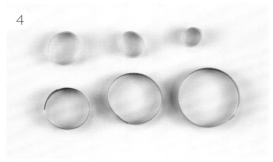

Make six ring coils, from big to small, with light brown and medium yellow strips.

Process the six ring coils into pentagonal coils by pinching.

| 6 | 7 |

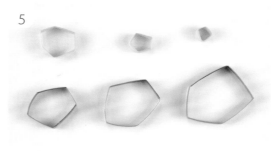

Put these six pentagonal coils together from big to small.

According to the method of steps 4 to 6, make eight groups of polygon coils, which are triangles, quadrilaterals, and pentagons.

| 8 | 9 |

Make two sets of curved line combinations and three curved leaf loops with black strips for claws, and make a tight coil with black strip for the eye.

Make curved lines, crescent coil, and curved leaf loop with lemon yellow strips. Make a black tight coil for the eye of the little tortoise.

10

Put these elements together to make a little tortoise.

11

In the center of the background paper, add the jade green crescent, then arrange the square coils along the crescent curve as the edge of the tortoise shell.

12

On the edge of the tortoise shell, add several groups of polygonal coils.

13

Continue to add polygonal coils to form a complete tortoise shell.

14

Add the head and tail of the tortoise in front of and behind the shell.

15

Add tortoise feet under the shell.

16

On the feet of the tortoise, add the claws, and add the eye on the head.

17

Add a small tortoise to the shell of the big tortoise. Adjust the picture, fix it with glue, and the work is done.

7. Goldfish (for Wealth and Knowledge)

The Chinese phrase "gold and jade fill the hall" comes from the Taoist classic *Lao Zi* (or *Lao Tzu*), which refers to lots of wealth as well as knowledge. "Gold-jade" and "gold fish" are homophonic in Chinese, so in traditional Chinese auspicious patterns, people often use goldfish to imply "gold and jade in full."

    In this work, the artist creates two vivid goldfish on paper. They are waving their long tails, chasing each other and playing together. Two clusters of green water plants beside the goldfish not only depict the watery environment in which the goldfish live, but also enrich and harmonize the color of the work.

Colors and Elements

Tails	●	basic crescent, S crescent, S loop
Back	●	crescent
Bodies and upper eyelids	● ● ◗	crescent
Fins	●	curved leaf loop, S loop
Mouths	●	marquise coil
Eyes	●	crescent coil
Patterns	●	loose coil
Water plants	●	crescent, S crescent
Background	white watercolor paper (suggested size: 30 cm × 20 cm)	

1

Take the deep red strip and make a fat S crescent as shown in the picture, forming a goldfish tail.

2

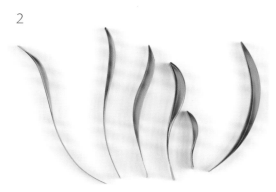

Scrape the two ends of the basic loops with a bamboo knife to form S loops. Make altogether six S loops, S crescents and crescents with deep red strips.

3

Fill these elements in the S crescent tail.

4

Make seven goldfish tails of different shapes as shown in the picture.

5

Make a basic crescent with deep red strip, and then glue its two ends and pinch out two right angles as the back of one goldfish.

6

Take pink, flesh color and deep red strips to make the upper eyelids and bodies of two goldfish in the shape of crescent.

7

Make one curved leaf loop and two S loops with deep red strips for the fins.

8

Use black strips to make four crescent coils as the eyes, and use deep red strips to make two marquise coils for the mouth.

9

Make eight loose coils with deep red strips for the patterns of one goldfish.

10

Make crescents and S crescents as shown in the picture with grass green strips as the water plants.

11

On the right side of the background, lay out the back, body, and mouth of the first goldfish.

12

Continue to piece out the body and fin of the goldfish.

13

Add a tail.

14

Lay out the second goldfish on the left side of the first goldfish.

15

Add fin and tail to the second goldfish.

16

Place patterns on the left goldfish.

17

Fill the black eyes in the blisters of the two goldfish.

18

At the top right of the background, lay out the first clump of water plants.

19

On the left side of the background, lay out the second clump of water plants. Adjust the picture, fix it with glue, and the work is done.

8. Bat and Deer (for Luck and Fortune)

Luck, Fortune, and Longevity are the three gods in Chinese folk belief. In Chinese, "luck" and "bat" are homophones, so people use bats to represent Luck; "fortune" and "deer" are homophones, so people use deer to represent Fortune; and the peach is fruit for immortals in Chinese legend, so people use peaches to represent Longevity. Bat, deer, and peach are combined to represent happiness, wealth, and longevity.

In this work, the author harmoniously combines a swift bat, a lovely deer, and a plump peach through ingenious composition and skillful techniques to place the good morals of "luck, fortune, and longevity."

Colors and Elements

Element	Colors	Shapes
Deer body parts	●	crescent, hook crescent
Deer feet	●	crescent
Antlers	●	hook crescent, curved leaf loop
Deer eye	● ●	loose coil, marquise coil
Copper coin patterns	◡	marquise coil, ring coil
Bat	● ●	teardrop coil, tight coil
Bat wings	●	basic crescent, wave crescent
Peach	● ●	basic crescent
Branch and leaves	● ●	curved leaf loop
Background	white watercolor paper (suggested size: 30 cm × 20 cm)	

1

Take the light brown strips and make crescents as the parts of the deer's body.

2

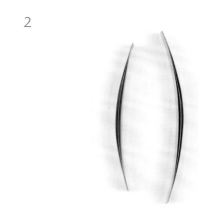

Make two long crescents with light brown strips.

3

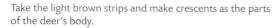

Combine the two long crescents as the deer's leg, and make four legs in total.

4

Use light brown strips to make two hook crescents as the antlers. Make four curved leaf loops as the bifurcated antlers.

5

Use black and light brown strips to make a loose coil and a marquise coil as the deer's eye.

6

Make one ring coil and four marquise coils with medium yellow strips, and put four marquise coils into the ring coil to form a copper coin. Make four copper coins altogether.

7

Make two teardrop coils with red strips for the head and body of the bat, and then make two tight coils with khaki strips as bat eyes.

8

Make two basic crescents and two wave crescents with red strips as the bat wings.

9

Put all the parts together into a complete bat.

10

Take pink and light pink strips and make two basic crescents as peaches; take mint green strips and make two curved leaf loops as peach leaves. Take light brown strips and make a curved leaf loop as the branch.

11

Combine the fruit, leaves, and branch into a complete peach.

12

On the top left of the background, lay out the head and ear of the deer. Continue to lay out the neck and body of the deer.

13

Put together the limbs of the deer. Add antlers to its head.

14

Add the eye and the copper coin patterns on the body.

15

Add a bat above the head of the deer. Put the peach next to the mouth of the deer. Adjust the picture, fix it with glue, and the work is done.

9. Phoenix (for Harmony)

"Phoenix facing the sun," a metaphor for talented people catching up with good opportunities, is one of the traditional auspicious patterns in China. The phoenix is a sacred bird in ancient Chinese legends. It is the king of birds and the bird of auspiciousness. It symbolizes harmony, perfection, and a bright future.

In this work, the artist uses orange and red to delineate the phoenix and the rising sun, showing vigorous vitality and a bright future. The whole work is exquisite in composition, brilliant in color, auspicious and festive.

Colors and Elements

Phoenix body	●	crescent, *ruyi*-shaped coil
Tail	●	curved line
Tail feathers	●	basic loop, transformed loop
Head	● ○ ●	teardrop coil
Feathers on body	● ●	marquise coil, loose coil
The rising sun	● ●	loose coil, ring coil, teardrop coil
Background	white watercolor paper (suggested size: 30 cm × 20 cm)	

1

Take the deep red strip, fold it in half, and scrape out the radian with a bamboo knife.

2

Adjust the length of the two ends of the strip by pulling, so that there is a space between two pieces of strip.

3

Turn the strip over and scrape the reverse arc with a bamboo knife at the tail.

4

Cut out the excess paper and glue it to form the *ruyi*-shaped coil.

5

Use deep red strips to make *ruyi*-shaped coils and crescents like those shown in the picture to form the main body of the phoenix.

6

Using deep red strips to make three curved lines with the end glued to form a loop for the main part of the tail plume of the phoenix.

7

Make a large number of transformed loops with deep red strips as feathers for the tail.

8

Make a teardrop coil with black, white, and deep red strips for the head of the phoenix.

9

Take deep red and orange strips to make three basic loops for feathers at the end of the phoenix tail.

10

Use deep red and orange strips to make three marquise coils respectively for feathers on the phoenix body.

11

Make nine loose coils with orange strips as another type of feathers.

12

Make a loose coil with deep red strips as the center of the rising sun. Make a ring coil with deep red and orange strips as the rim of the rising sun.

13

Use deep red and orange strips to make twelve teardrop coils for patterns inside the rising sun.

14

Fill twelve teardrop coils in the sun frame.

15

On the top of the background, lay out the head of the phoenix.

16

Continue to lay out the body. Under the body, add its tail plumes.

17

Add feathers to the tail plumes.

18

On the phoenix body, add marquise coil feathers. On the tail plumes, add basic loop feathers.

19

Continue to add loose coil feathers on its body. On the left side of the phoenix, add the rising sun. Adjust the picture, fix it with glue, and the work is done.

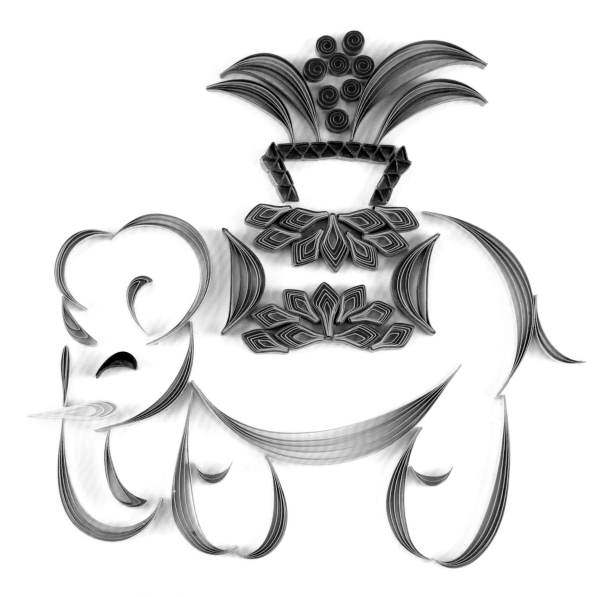

10. Elephant (for Peace)

"Elephant with vase" is a traditional Chinese auspicious pattern, implying peace in the world and a harvest of grains. Thick and steady, elephant is an auspicious animal. Chinese character of "elephant" is homophone for the character of "auspicious." The character of "vase" is a homophone for the character of "peace." Therefore, in the traditional Chinese auspicious pattern, the elephant laden with treasure vase implies a world in peace.

In this work, the artist uses the medium gray crescents to create a charmingly naive elephant. It wears brocade and looks graceful and luxurious. It carries a treasure vase on its back, with flowers in the vase, symbolizing peace and prosperity of the whole world. This festive work is exquisite in composition and bright in color.

Colors and Elements

Element	Color	Technique
Elephant body parts	●	crescent, curved leaf loop
Tusk	○	basic loop
Eye	●	curved leaf loop
Brocade	● ● ○ ● ●	basic crescent, diamond loop
Vase	●	combination of broken lines
Evergreen flowers	●	loose coil
Evergreen leaves	● ● ● ●	basic crescent
Background		white watercolor paper (suggested size: 30 cm × 20 cm)

1

Use medium gray strips to make the crescents and curved leaf loops as shown in the picture to form parts of the elephant body.

2

Make a basic loop with flesh color strip for the tusk, and make a curved leaf loop with black strip for the elephant's eye.

3

Use grass green, orange, lemon yellow, orange red, deep red, and pink strips to make two crescents for the brocade.

4

Make a basic loop with grass green, orange, lemon yellow, orange red, deep red and pink strips.

5

Flatten the basic loop vertically.

6

Turn the basic loop back to its original shape and flatten it again horizontally.

7

Organize the basic loop to form a diamond loop.

8

Make eighteen such diamond loops.

9

Take a burnt umber strip and fold it every 0.5 cm twice.

10

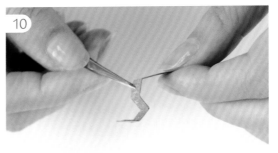

Reverse the strip and fold it every 0.5 cm twice.

11

Bind the folded strips with glue into two continuous equilateral triangles.

12

Continue to follow this approach and make several contiguous equilateral triangles.

13

Make three continuous equilateral triangles, two short and one long for the vase.

14

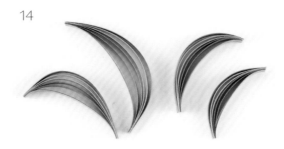

Use grass green, olive green, apple green, and jade green strips to make four crescents for evergreen leaves.

15

Make eight loose coils with deep red strips for evergreen flowers.

16

On the left side of the background, lay out the head of the elephant.

17

Underneath the elephant's head, lay out its trunk.

18

Continue to lay out the rump and abdomen of the elephant.

19

Put the legs of the elephant under its body.

20

Add the ears to the head, wrinkles to the skin around the joints in the legs, and add the tail to the rump of the elephant.

21

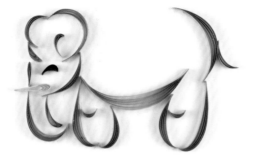

Add the eye and tusk to the elephant.

22

On the elephant's back, piece together the lower part of the brocade with diamond loops.

23

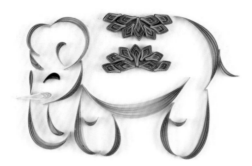

Continue to use the diamond loops to piece together the upper part of the brocade.

24

On both sides of brocade patterns, add the brocade frame.

25

Put the vase together over the brocade.

26

Insert evergreen leaves and flowers in the vase. Adjust the picture, fix it with glue, and the work is done.